COWBOY
BANDANAS

COWBOY BANDANAS
USES & ABUSES

LEE THOMSON
ILLUSTRATED BY JIM LEWIS

GIBBS·SMITH
P
PUBLISHER

SALT LAKE CITY

First edition
95 94 93 10 9 8 7 6 5 4 3 2 1

This is a Peregrine Smith Book, published by
Gibbs Smith, Publisher
P.O. Box 667
Layton, UT 84041

Design by Mary Ellen Thompson, TTA Design
Manufactured by Regent Publishing Services, Hong Kong

Library of Congress Cataloging-in-Publication Data
Thomson, Lee.
Cowboy bandanas: uses and abuses / Lee Thomson; Jim Lewis, illustrator.
p. cm.
ISBN 0-87905-552-9
1. Cowboys—West (U.S.)—Humor. 2. Bandanas—Humor. I. Lewis, Jim. II. Title.
F596.T46 1993
978—dc20   92-43507
                            CIP

**TO MY FATHER AND MOTHER,
DR. WOODRUFF C. THOMSON
AND IRENE G. THOMSON**

FOREWORD

Few things will ever have the enduring popularity of the bandana. Americans have taken this humble square of printed cloth to heart. As part of the cowboy's outfit, the bandana has become a national symbol of individualism and self-reliance.

Some folks call the bandana a "101" because, they say, it has one hundred and one uses. The true number of uses are only limited by the human mind. There will always be at least one more way to put the bandana to work, because it has the freedom to function as needed by each person it serves.

There are so many practical, fun and sometimes off the wall uses for the bandana. Sure there are other items which could do a specific job better. Some of the suggested ideas would require a lot of bandanas or ones which are larger than the common modern 22-inch-sided model (older bandanas reached two to three feet per side). But that's not the point. Like a good old B western, nitpicking details should not stand in the way of a good story.

This is the story of the cowboy's bandana and its uses, both past and present—with some detours, of course. This book is not a simple list. The uses are woven into the narrative. It is left up to each reader to add up just how many uses have been compiled here.

WHAT IS A BANDANA?

Bandanas are always bold, strong colors. Fighting colors. Nobody holds up a bandana to surrender. No sir. That job is left to some sissy white hankie.

A bandana is a square piece of cloth with an attitude. It sends a message, good or bad, but never indifferent. That band of color 'round a hero's neck tells you he will stand for what's right even when he stands alone. A triangle of color riding over the nose and just under the cold eyes of a desperado tells you to reach for the sky and say your prayers.

Bandanas have always done the job for every American who has ever broken a sweat. Ever since colonial times, bandanas have been worn and used for their color and classy cussedness.

LIFE AND THE BANDANA

A REAL COWBOY RIDES THROUGH LIFE WITH A BANDANA. AT THE TRAILHEAD, BANDANA LIGATURES TIE OFF THE COWBABY'S UMBILICAL CORD. HIS DADDY'S BANDANA MAY BE THE ONLY DIAPER HE'LL EVER HAVE. AT TRAIL'S END, ONE BANDANA WILL TIE HIS SLACK JAW SHUT WHILE ANOTHER COVERS HIS FACE. IN BETWEEN, A COWBOY AND HIS BANDANA COVER A LOT OF TERRITORY TOGETHER. ALONG THE TRAIL THE BANDANA COVERS A LOT OF THE COWBOY.

ON THE TRAIL

Doesn't it sound exciting to take part in a cattle drive? Oh, to be part of the romance and history of the Old West! A ride along the Goodnight-Loving Trail just has to be a great time. Its name has such a nice ring to it.

Okay, stop! It's reality-check time, but only for just a minute. The world of a real 1870s cowboy was one of hard work, boredom, and occasional terror best viewed from our late-20th-century armchairs. Do you still want to be a cowboy? Here's your job.

Your hours are from can't see to can't see with split night duty. The heat and cold come free and you get all the dust you can eat. You get a shower when it rains and a bath when there's some muddy river to swim with half-wild longhorns. Your sleeping accommodations will always have precisely the right-sized rocks poking in your back. And just the right party mix of critters that crawl, creep or fly will keep you company.

Your menu will be full of variety—as long as you like to eat beans and sourdough in an intimate firelight atmosphere. You can also widen your circle of friends. Think of the renegades, rustlers, cardsharps and whores you will probably meet. You will certainly get on a first-name basis with cantankerous horses and contrary cows.

Wages? If you got more than two-bit pay, you'd just lose it gambling.

Benefits? You want vacation days? Hell, this is a vacation. After all, it's your fantasy.

How about retirement? The boys will surely dig you a grave deep enough to keep the coyotes away. And the marker comes free. Maybe someone knows his letters and can write a note to your kin.

Do you still want to go on that trail ride? What, you still think it might be interesting? All right, let's go. But first let's lay in our provisions. Be sure to bring a whole passel of bandanas. You'll need 'em. This ain't going to be no picnic, y'know. You and your bandana will have plenty of chances to show your true colors.

TRAILHEAD

A drive always starts with good spirits and high hopes—some call it high hat. The boss looks to bring every single cow in for top dollar at the railhead. Every cowboy is already counting his wages and figuring how to spend them.

All equipment is in good repair and clothes are clean. The cattle are well fed and watered. They act like they'd gladly go wherever you want, if only you'd kindly point the way.

Shorty has a new ready-made shirt on—one size sort of fits all. He uses bandanas as arm garters so his hands are free.

It's time to move out. Soon the sun is hot enough to make you glad a bandana shades the back of your neck. Your bandana is quickly put to work as a dust mask because you draw duty riding drag (a scary connotation to the modern urban reader).

Nothing much goes on the first day. You are bored already. After all, look at the company you keep. Cows are stupid. If this keeps up it will drive you crazy. Why else do cowboys yodel? You need something to fill your time. Put a rock in your bandana and pretend you're David and that lizard is Goliath. You missed. Well, practice will pass the time. At least you didn't hit yourself.

You are a greenhorn and there's a lot to learn. It's easy to practice your knots with your bandana as you plod along. Let's see, the rabbit comes out of the hole, goes around the trees and. . . .

I AM FROM MONTANA

I WEAR A BANDANA

MY SPURS THEY ARE SILVER

MY HAIR IT IS GRAY

—OLD CHILDREN'S SONG

CAMP

It's been a long day. Time to make camp. You have to help Cookie fix the grub because you're low man. Nobody'd better complain about the cooking or they'll go hungry. You grab the skillet handle with your bandana and pull it off the fire. The coffee's so thick you need your bandana strainer. Squat by the campfire while you eat. Don't even think of spreading a bandana on the ground and sitting on it. After dinner you use an old bandana to clean those sticky beans and coffee grounds from your tin plate and cup. After breakfast you do the same thing.

You have some time to your self. Heat water in the coffeepot, dip your bandana in and use it to clean up a little. Every night that warmth will feel better to your aching bones. Tex offers you a drink. You wipe the bottle mouth with your bandana. Take off your boots and clean out the toe jam.

You go over to your saddlebags. On your way you see Cookie using bandanas to tie food bags from the limbs so animals won't get in them.

You take a bandana bundle out and open it. You gaze at your sweetheart's picture and take a deep breath of her favorite perfume. She splashed it on the bandana just before you left. It makes you a little homesick and you feel like playing some sad music. Shoot, she forgot to pack your harmonica. Well, cover your comb with your bandana and fake it.

You go out and check on your horse. When forage gets sparser, you may want to put a bandana hobble on her so she can graze at night.

Now it's time to turn in. There's more of the same and then some tomorrow.

STILL ON THE TRAIL

Days go by. You learn fast that the cowboy's life is an elemental one. Earth, wind, fire and ice all seem to fight over the privilege of taking you down. You and the good Lord are sharing the same roof. That must suit Him, but it gets to your bones.

The herd's hoofs turn the ground into powder which finds its way into everything. You wrap your few personal effects and keepsakes in a bandana to keep the dust out. If the wind doesn't blow up a dust storm, it brings slanting rain which turns the powder to muck. Your bandana wipes off the muck and manure flicked up on your face. You hope the clouds break soon.

The summer sun, they say, can fry a man's brains. Heat stroke and dehydration can certainly kill a person. A wetted bandana to wipe your face and put back on your neck sure feels good.

The heat starts to get to the men and livestock. This is the dry part of the trail. It's another twenty miles to water. When you finally reach the water hole, the thirst-crazed cattle want it more than you do and beat you to it. Strain the water through your bandana so you'll gulp fewer surprises.

If it isn't too hot, it's too cold. A cattle drive in the spring or autumn can catch a freak storm of sleet and snow. The bandana keeps your neck a little warmer. When a norther blows down the high plains, you might as well be in Siberia. The tumbleweeds are the biggest wind break between the North Pole and North Texas. If your hat weren't tied down by your bandana, it would blow off and roll clear to Galveston.

At night you can take some rocks from the campfire ring, wrap them in a bandana, and put them between your blankets for added warmth.

If the weather doesn't get you, the flora and fauna will (no, those aren't two dance hall girls). Every brush and branch wants a piece of you. That last one got your bandana instead of your neck. But don't think your bandana will save you from everything. Careful, that Spanish bayonet cuts right through leather and bandanas too.

Every critter that can bite, sting or buzz seems to find you. Wearing a bandana around your neck and flicking another with one hand helps to control the horseflies, deerflies, blackflies, no-see-ums, mosquitoes and who knows what else.

Some day you'll want to settle down, marry and have a little boy named Deet, and you will tell him, "Deet, grow up and be a scientist, not a cowboy, and figure out some potion to get these bugs off!"

Everything tears and tatters. Equipment breaks. Nerves fray. Out here there are no stores and few spare parts. You just fix things the best you can. A bandana can replace a strap so you can keep your chaps around your legs. As a lash or lace, it'll do if need be. You can even use a bandana as a rein or short lead. You're in real sorry shape if you have to use one as a makeshift stirrup.

It's a good thing a cowboy and his bandana don't break easily.

STAMPEDE

It's your turn to pull night watch. Not much is happening, but the cattle seem edgy. There's some dry lightning off yonder, and some coyotes or other varmints are rustling in the underbrush, but that's nothing unusual.

Suddenly it just happens. The herd jerks into motion. Was it thunder? Renegades? Rustlers? Who knows. Maybe it's just a cow gone crazy with flies in her eyes and nose or some steer's flatulence. Cows don't need a reason. If Bessie starts running, Bossie thinks it's a good idea, too.

This is not the time to use your bandana. No one's going to cheer "Olé!" if you stand in front of the herd and wave a red bandana.

Raise the alarm and get everybody moving.

The herd decides it would be fun to tip over Cookie's wagon (this herd instinct is still alive in the 20th century except cars and football goalposts seem to be the preferred targets).

The bandana goes to work after the stampede is headed off. Pete was knocked off his horse and broke his leg. The boys help Cookie set Pete's leg and splint it with bandanas and a board from Cookie's wagon.

Cookie's wagon is pulled back upright and all the scattered pots and stuff are put back in a way to leave room for Pete. Now it's time to round up strays and get ready to move on.

All of a sudden you could stand a little boredom.

EUREKA!

AFTER THE STAMPEDE YOU GO AFTER STRAYS. YOU FOLLOW A COUPLE UP A CANYON. THE TRAIL LEADS ALONG A PRETTY LITTLE STREAM CALLED CHERRY OR CRIPPLE CREEK OR SOMETHING. AFTER A WHILE IT'S TIME TO STOP FOR A DRINK. AS YOU BEND OVER, YOU SEE A FLASH OF COLOR IN THE WATER. GOLD! YOU FIND A NUGGET AS BIG AS A BULLET. DRAW A MAP ON YOUR BANDANA AND BUNDLE YOUR GOLD IN IT. TUCK IT AWAY. FOR NOW, THIS IS YOUR LITTLE SECRET.

"MY COWBOYING DAYS ARE OVER," YOU THINK. "EASY STREET, HERE I COME!"

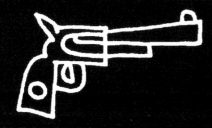 # AMBUSH

Shorty found more than strays. He races back into camp with renegades closing in on his tail. At first everyone thinks they should circle the wagon, but that doesn't work, so you all hightail it to some big rocks. Poor Pete's a little slow with his crutches and all. He catches an arrow in the shoulder. Luckily it's only a flesh wound.

The renegades run off a few beeves, but otherwise the herd is okay. Cookie doubles as company surgeon. The arrowhead isn't in too far, and Cookie thinks he can get it. He gives Pete a shot of whiskey and a bandana to bite down on. Cookie wraps a bandana around his hand for a better grip, puts his boot on Pete's sternum, and yanks for all he's worth. Another surgical success. Cookie folds a bandana and tells you to put pressure on Pete's wound to stop the bleeding. When it stops bleeding, make him a bandana sling and tie another bandana around his chest to hold his arm.

You take the arrowhead and put it in your bandana bundle as another souvenir. It's a good thing this drive is almost over.

SNAKEBIT

One more night and you'll be in town. The boys are getting rambunctious. Jess and Buck find a little rattler and toss it back and forth on sticks. Of course the game gets out of hand. The snake is tossed a little too far and lands on poor old Pete, who's lying there by the fire.

Cookie's there in a flash. He wipes his knife on his bandana before he cuts an X over the puncture mark and starts to suck and spit. He whips on a tourniquet and tells you and Shorty to help Pete get into town to the doc.

Pete's running a fever. Is it caused by infection in the wound, by the venom, or both? Try to cool him down with a wet bandana on his brow.

As the boys load Pete up, you cut the rattles off the snake and put another souvenir in your bandana bundle.

Pete's in a bad way. You'd better hurry.

TRAIL'S END

Pete made it to the doc but he's not yet out of the woods, if you know what I mean. The rest of the boys brought the herd into the stockyard. Each cowboy draws his pay and, with a whoop and a holler, heads off to spend it.

The boys get into their saddlebags and pull out their bandana bundles to get combs, clean shirts (or at least clean collars) and other necessaries for a night on the town. Each saves his best bandana for this celebration. Some of the boys head for Jake's Saloon; others go straight for Roxy's sporting house. But not you. Sorry, you're the straight-shootin' hero of this piece.

First you have some business to attend to. You look up the assayer. "What's that, Mr. Assayer, fool's gold? Isn't that just a cowboy's luck."

Now you aren't in much of a mood to celebrate. Maybe a hot bath will soak your tired bones and wash your troubles, not to mention weeks of trail dust, away. You check into a hotel and order a bathtub. You cover your face with a hot, moist bandana, close your eyes, and just soak for heaven knows how long. You'll sleep in a real bed tonight, but first get dressed and go out for a while. Pull out the bandana bundle your sweetheart fixed up for you. The arrowhead and snake rattles make you wonder how Pete's doing. Those "nuggets" were going to be your future. But you don't linger on those thoughts. There's your sweetheart's picture. Tonight you'll keep it in your breast pocket. Tie on the bandana she gave you. Go down to Jake's, order a sarsaparilla and find an empty table in a corner.

Before you settle down, Shorty comes over and tells you that Jess and Buck were at it again. Seems they got full of the devil after drinking red-eye and decided to have a shooting contest. Jess tied a bandana over Buck's eyes and challenged Buck to shoot a bottle off some passed-out drunk's head. Buck pulled out his hog leg and fired. The drunk and the bottle are okay, but the bullet flew out the window in the direction of the doctor's office. A bunch of the boys have gone over to check on Pete.

Jake's is crowded and noisy, but you don't notice. Even the thick smoke can't keep you from smelling her favorite perfume on your bandana. Your thoughts beat you home, but, Lord willing, you won't be far behind.

FIRST AID

Whenever medical help is not close by, the bandana is first in any first-aid kit. It can be used to cover wounds, stop bleeding or immobilize a limb. Depending how you use a bandana, it can be called a bandage, compress, tourniquet, sling, splint tie, eye patch, or ankle wrap. A cool, wet bandana fights a fever. A warm, damp bandana soothes a sore neck. Around the house a bandana can hold ice packs or hot pads wherever they are needed. And as a first-

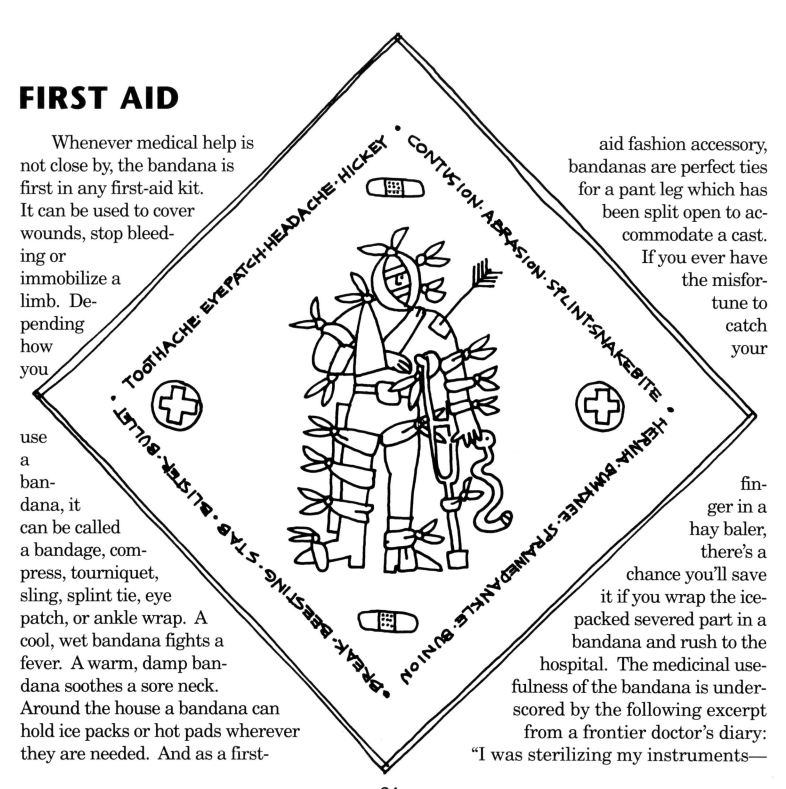

aid fashion accessory, bandanas are perfect ties for a pant leg which has been split open to accommodate a cast. If you ever have the misfortune to catch your finger in a hay baler, there's a chance you'll save it if you wrap the ice-packed severed part in a bandana and rush to the hospital. The medicinal usefulness of the bandana is underscored by the following excerpt from a frontier doctor's diary: "I was sterilizing my instruments—

both of them—when some cowboys carried in the most suffering, sorrowful-looking creature I'd ever seen in my life. He was covered head to foot in bandanas. The sight roused my natural curiosity, so I asked the remarkably lucid patient what had happened.

"'Pete's m'name, Doc,' he said. 'I'm a feller on a considerable streak of bad luck. We was bringin' some longhorns up from Texas and it wasn't but a few days out when the whole danged herd decided to stampede right over me. The cusses knocked me off my horse and I broke my leg. I had to borry some bandanas to splint my leg.

"'Then wouldn't ya know it, just the next day while the boys was roundin' up strays, renegades hit us and I catched an arrow in my shoulder. That made me borry another bandana for a sling.

"'Things seemed to settle down until last night, when some of the boys tossed a rattler on me. It was all accidental-like, but that didn't make no nevermind to the snake. It bit me just the same. So I had to borry more bandanas for a tourniquet and such.

"'On the way in I musta fainted or somethin', 'cause I fell off my horse and got kicked in the head. That explains this here gash. That was the last bandana I borryed, unless'n you count the bandanas the boys used to tie me back on my horse.

"'You can understand I've been a bit deelerious from the festerin' wounds and snakebite 'n' such, so you'll pardon me if I can't tell you exactly how many bandanas I'm sporting.

"'Y'know, Doc, after this I'm givin' up cowboyin' for poker. I figger all my bad luck's used up. The only thing I ain't had on this ride is a bullet in my britches.'

"The spirit of the caduceus o'ertook me, and I went to work. I pulled out my very own bandana and dried off my instruments. I then poured ether on the bandana and anesthetized the patient.

"His story is truly the most remarkable tale ever heard in this territory. I would not have believed him if I had not seen him with my own eyes.

"The patient is resting now while I catch up on some paperwork. He is certainly lucky to be alive. His survival must be attributed to prompt and proper applications of bandanas to immobilize his leg, stop bleeding and retard the spread of venom. Although fever and infection persist and are complicated by the snake bite, I remain hopeful.

"A gunshot just went off. I must go check on the patient."

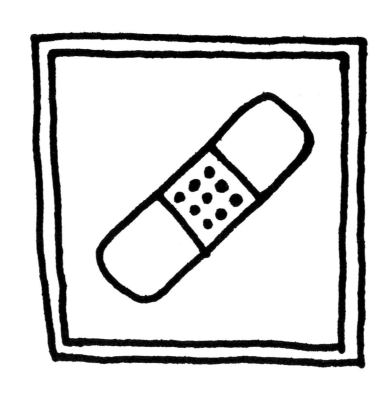

BANDANA MALPRACTICE TIPS

1) IF YOU ENCOUNTER AN EMERGENCY, GET COMPETENT MEDICAL HELP AS SOON AS POSSIBLE. DON'T PULL YOUR BANDANA OVER YOUR MOUTH AND NOSE AND PRETEND YOU ARE A FIELD SURGEON.

2) USE A BANDANA AS A TOURNIQUET ONLY FOR DRAMATIC EFFECT IN A BOOK OR MOVIE. DON'T USE A TOURNIQUET ON A LIVE PERSON.

SORRY,
THE OPEN RANGE IS CLOSED
PLEASE DETOUR

YOU'VE HAD ENOUGH EXCITEMENT TO LAST A SPELL. LET'S
EXPLORE HOW BANDANAS ARE WORN AND USED TODAY.

ANATOMY AND THE BANDANA

THE HEADBONE'S . . .

The bandana's home is where the head is. All types of people wear one as a headcover or sweatband. Some might say the bandana is the class of the head. *We* don't make puns like that.

Wear a bandana in a triangle fold atop your head and you can be anyone. Add an earring and choose from a) a pirate; b) a rock star; c) a biker; d) a gang member; e) a gypsy; or f) all of the above. A football player stays cool and comfortable by wearing the same style.

An enterprising cowboy can make a swamp cooler by wearing his straw hat over a bandana. Wetted either by water or sweat, he gets evaporative cooling.

Either the triangle fold or the more daring knotted four-corner style can make a heck of a sun bonnet for a bald guy at the beach.

Want to be the hit of the costume party? Pin a couple of braided gray hairpieces to your sweatband and go as a famous pigtailed country-and-western recording artist.

Take a yuppie. Let's call her Mary Ellen. Let her drive her Volvo to her health club/fern bar and carry her Gucci gym bag into the dressing room. Even though she wears the latest name-of-the-month shoes and workout clothes, she won't step out of the dressing room without a regular ol' bandana sweatband on. Why? It's the only real status symbol she has.

The bandana is a hat saver. A new bandana hatband will get a little more mileage out of the ol' Stetson. And with a little bandana padding, the cardsharp can get some use out of that fancy hat he just won off that swellheaded dude.

The cowboy's least favorite version of bandana headwear meant a trip to the jawbreaker. Why would a cowboy tie a bandana around his face when he had a toothache? Maybe it let everyone know that they had better back off.

. . . CONNECTED TO THE NECKBONE

Just about everything humans have hung around their necks has been pretty damn useless. But what can they do except choke you if they get entangled in machinery?

The bandana is the utilitarian exception. It's anything but useless neckwear.

As a neckpiece, the bandana does more than just add decorative color. It protects you from whatever threatens to bite, burn or scratch. But that's not all.

People have a lot to hide when it comes to their necks. Cowboys of the 1800s wore such lousy collars that they needed to wear a bandana just for self respect. Today people who end up wearing part of their lunch can make it through the day by wearing a bandana over the gravy stains on their shirts. And don't forget the neck itself. When did you last wash your neck? Do you have a hickey, wrinkles, or an oversized Adam's apple? Is your chin better described in the plural? Do you feel anxious around Thanksgiving, turkey neck? If so, there's a bandana for you.

WOMEN AND THE BANDANA

THE COWBOY IS NO MATCH FOR THE COWGIRL AND HER CITY COUSIN WHEN IT COMES TO PUTTING THE BANDANA TO USE. YOU WOULD THINK THAT, AFTER ALL THOSE YEARS SPENT ON THE TRAIL, GOING DAYS AND NIGHTS ON END WEARING THE SAME CLOTHES AND HAVING SUCH LIMITED ROOM IN HIS SADDLEBAGS, THE COWBOY WOULD HAVE AT LEAST FIGURED OUT THE MOST BASIC PRINCIPLE OF BANDANA WEAR. BUT HE NEVER DID. EVERY WOMAN, HOWEVER, KNOWS INSTINCTIVELY THAT THE SECRET TO ANY LIMITED WARDROBE IS TO

ACCESSORIZE! ACCESSORIZE! ACCESSORIZE!

AROUND HER HAIR SHE TIED A . . .

The world-famous expert on women's fashion and truck upholstery, Gilbert of Show Low, tells us a bandana is a basic necessity for every woman's hair because it adds just the right splash of color while it does its job.

The sporting woman wouldn't be caught dead in her aerobics class or on the racquetball court without her bandana rolled thin and tied across her forehead. There's nothing better to hold a ponytail or pigtails. And, with a thicker fold which is tied from the top of the head down back behind the ears, the bandana makes a colorful hairband.

Folded neatly as a triangle, the bandana is a smart and handy headcovering. Housecleaning needn't muss the hair as long as you wear your bandana tied on the top in the chic and famous Lucy Do. A knot behind the ears tells everyone you are not afraid to make the strong Babushka fashion statement. Tied snugly under your chin, your bandana lets you cruise 90 MPH in your Cadillac convertible and not have to rerat a single hair in your beehive. And last, but not least, would anyone be around to hear "Attention, K-Mart shoppers . . ." if you didn't have a bandana to cover those curlers? Don't forget the sleek turban look, either. Mix and match. Experiment. You're sure to find just the right look for you.

BANDANA FASHION

We asked Gilbert of Show Low to take us down the runways of bandana fashion.

"Thank you. Bandanas are just soooo versatile. Don't you just love them to death?

"Slim and Shirley give us our first glimpse of bandana fashion.

"Slim brings us the latest in formal bandana wear, the cowboy tuxedo. The number of rhinestones is cut way back this year in order to focus on the flashy bandana cummerbund. Slim also wears a matching bandana neckerchief tied rakishly at the side of his neck à la young John Wayne. A third bandana adds color to the breast pocket. Our formal menswear has been so successful that we will be adding women's formal and wedding wear lines next year.

"Shirley's ensemble has a triangle fold theme. Her bandana is worn Boy Scout style about her neck so she can be prepared for the ever-changing fashion range wars. That same bandana, knotted loosely, can either be draped over one shoulder or turned full front for two completely different looks. That last look can help with a neckline that's a little more daring than you are.

"Shirley continues the theme with another bandana triangle knotted on her side.

"Hoot is next with the trail look. His bandana is tied at the back of the neck to allow quick and easy face covering. You never know when a dust storm's coming or a stagecoach needs robbing.

"Hoot's Levis were authentically ripped on genuine barbed wire. The more revealing tears were tastefully mended 'dogpatch' style with different-colored bandanas.

"Out on the trail that spare bandana comes in handy for more than just a bad hair day. Say a rustler's bullet leaves a nasty hole in your new jacket. No problem. Your bandana can cover that hole. What if your saddle pony breaks down and you're forty miles from water? Your bandana can tie your canteen to your belt and adds a flash of color as you walk.

"Tatiana shows us that a bandana rolled thin works either plain, twisted or braided whether you wear it around your neck; as a belt; as an armlet, bracelet or anklet; or tied around the thigh.

"Last and certainly least, in terms of square inches, Molly models the ever-popular bandana bikini. What's that, Molly? No pockets? Fold a bandana and tie it to a bandana belt for a fanny pack that has plenty of room for your lotion and paperback. Will this girl ever get off the beach? If she does, that halter top with a pair of jeans looks just as great at home as on the back of a Harley.

"There is a bandana breechcloth and belt ensemble which we are not modeling today. It seems to be catching on with certain guys who are getting in touch with their manhood. Of course, that's something cowboys have never been out of touch with.

"Well, that's it for now. Let's give all our people a big hand. Thanks ever so much for coming. Ciao!"

(As the crowd is leaving, Gilbert is overheard saying, "C'mon, honey. Like I said up on the stage, let's go get some chow.")

IS THAT A BANDANA IN YOUR POCKET, OR . . .

One reason a cowboy wears his bandana around his neck is that it's downright uncomfortable in the saddle when you have a soggy lump of cloth in your back pocket. But when not riding, the back pocket is a good place to keep a bandana because it's easy to reach and easy to put back.

Ever since some wimpy 17th-century European dandies decided sticking tobacco up their noses was stylish, people have appreciated bandanas for serious nose maintenance. Cowboys use bandanas to wipe, but never to blow, their noses (that's what a finger and the ground are for). Any cold sufferer knows an old, soft, cotton bandana beats the heck out of a scratchy, flimsy paper tissue.

Sometimes how a bandana is worn in the back pocket is more important than how it is used. Didn't Grandpappy Amos first have his bandana trailing out of his overalls? So why do some kids think this is a cool look? Is it just a flash of color, or does it flash a message? Certain urban subcultures use the color or placement of a bandana to tell who or what the wearer is (enough said). Depending on your neck of the woods, you may need to be careful what you do with your bandana after you clean your glasses or wipe your nose.

THE BANDANA LOOKS SMART ON ANY SPECIES,
AND ANY SPECIES LOOKS SMART ON A BANDANA.

THE GREAT COMMUNICATOR

A bandana always sends a message.

How a bandana is worn or used is a message in itself. Tied to a tree, it can mark a trail. If tied to a door or tent flap, do not disturb!

A bandana can also be the messenger. As a writing pad, the bandana has its limitations. A bright bandana on a tree or bush does a better job calling attention to the paper note wrapped inside. A star-struck woman could write her phone number on her bandana and throw it up on the stage, but she'd probably get better results if she used one of her unmentionables.

As a printed message, bandanas have no limitations. A bandana can be printed with a message or slogan as easily as with a design.

Bandanas have carried political slogans since at least Martha Washington's time. Private enterprise exploits bandanas for their advertising potential. Bandanas are a popular souvenir of a place or event. Whole stadiums are filled with fans waving identical bandanas. We claim that the "homer hankie" as a full-fledged bandana.

Armbandanas have always been strong communicators. They're how you wear your heart on your sleeve.

No matter the message—when mourning, protesting, backing a kooky political cause or just playing war games—the bandana has the right color and pattern for you.

Bandanas are also educational. Some carry instructions for first-aid use. Some are maps. And others spell out the rules of a game.

As a flag, a bandana can put the message over when words will not do. In stealthy silence, a hunter can signal his party. In deafening noise, a signalman in the railyard can tell the engineer when to stop the train.

At great distances, a bandana in each hand can send the word by either semaphore or Morse code.

The drop of a bandana can start a horse race or a drag race.

Its bold colors make the bandana the perfect rally flag. People of common cause can quickly spot it amid the chaos and follow it out of trouble. That is how Japanese tourists are rounded up from airports and led to dude ranches.

All good things must come to an end. When parting is difficult, the bandana makes the goodbye last just a little bit longer as you ride out of sight.

HELPFUL HOMESTEAD HINTS

The bandana is every bit as useful indoors as it is outdoors. When you wipe that dribble off your chin with a paper tissue, do you think of all the needless deforestation you have caused? Have you read how much of America's landfills are bloated with paper products? Or are you just into all-natural products? It's time to break those paper product chains that bind you. The sturdy, soft, reusable bandana is for you.

Let's drop in on Aunt Mary Hazel. If there is a way to use a bandana around the house, Aunt Mary Hazel knows it.

Look in the kitchen. Those bandanas are really colorful napkins. There's a bandana over her bread dough while it's rising. Another one's covering her famous honey pie. Stubborn preserve jar lids always give when a bandana helper is applied. And a bandana is the only TV tray place mat you should use when watching those "Bonanza" reruns.

Aunt Mary Hazel has taught the hands bandana manners. Cowboy picnickers know that they can create the right mood for *amoré* if the correct chilled wine is wrapped in a bandana. The boys now wrap a bandana around cold drinks to avoid icy handshaking. And they would never put their long-neck bottles down without using a bandana coaster. When-

ever Auntie lets the boys in the parlor, she is sure to place bandana antimacassars on the backs and arms of the upholstered furniture.

Come on out to the living room. That bandana-wrapped frame around the picture of Butch and the gang is our favorite. Excuse me while I clean my glasses. Of course, I will use my bandana so the lenses won't get scratched. Oh, I see you are still using a bandana to mark your place in *Reader's Digest,* Auntie.

Aunt Mary Hazel has a real knack for sewing. Look at how she has all those bandana colors and patterns pieced together in this country tablecloth and that patchwork quilt. Right now she's making a braided bandana rug. She used to make clothes out of bandanas for the young'uns 'til they got old enough to be embarrassed. She sewed two bandanas together for that throw pillow, too. Please, Auntie, if you have a potpourri made out of a bandana, don't let us know about it.

Bandanas always play a major role in her holiday decorating. Her bandana bows, garlands and such make the perfect cowboy Christmas tree decorations. She has also learned this Japanese custom called *furoshiki* for wrapping presents in bandanas.

One of the first things Aunt Mary

Hazel taught me was that bandanas which are ready for the fashion pasture still have a lot of work left in them. A bandana can wash dishes and dry them, too. Whether cleaning windows and mirrors, dusting, polishing the silver on your turquoise jewelry, or shining boots, the bandana does the best job (bandana etiquette draws the line at cleaning toilets). Well, you get the idea. The bandana's a regular workhorse.

Well, we've gotta shove off. Thanks, Auntie. Catch you on the rebound.

THESE DAYS IT'S HARD TO TELL IF A BANDANA IS BEING WORN BY A GANG MEMBER OR A CHOIR BOY. THAT BANDANA-WEARING GUY WHO'S GETTING ON HIS HARLEY MIGHT BE A LAWYER OR AN OUTLAW BIKER. THEN AGAIN, HE MIGHT BE SOMEBODY RESPECTABLE. YOU JUST CAN'T ALWAYS JUDGE A BANDANA BY WHOM IT COVERS.

THE BANDANA AND THE BIGGEST HOUSEHOLD CHORE

Ladies, are you sick of cleaning up after the herd? Does your fella fancy himself a real workhorse, even though the glue factory'd reject him because he can't stick to anything?

Do your kids act like housework is cancer-causing or, worse yet, might be a sign of maturity? Try the handy dandy bandana.

So what really is the big lunk's problem? Lazy? Sure, but he's a man—and men think housework isn't manly. Hey, after all, it's your fault, right? You let him get away with this. Perhaps your feather duster is too frilly. Does it remind him of a French maid's uniform (which he'd rather see than wear)? Give him a bandana to do the job and tell him Randolph Scott'd be damn proud to see him working like this.

What's that? Your kids have never heard of Randolph Scott? Well, they've heard of C-R-A-C-K the whip! Kids know that a bandana-wielding mom means business. Careful now, don't hurt the little darlings. A damp bandana properly snapped approximately one inch from the behind is a great motivator. It just might relieve a little of Mom's stress, too.

BANDANAS AND THE MATERNAL INSTINCT

The bandana is an essential part of child rearing. If not for bandanas and mothers, we'd all be savages. Moms have always been there to dry a tear, wipe a nose or spit on a bandana corner and rub a face. Aw, Ma!

It was an old folk cure to dip a bandana corner in whiskey and rub it on the sore gums of a teething baby.

Mom's used to treat colds by rubbing Vicks VapoRub on the chest and tying a bandana over the goo.

Anyone who's actually been a mother knows the job ain't all it's cracked up to be. Many a bandana has been soaked with a mother's tears. Only another mother could understand the sight of a grown woman with bandanas stuffed in her ears. Aren't there studies about the relationship between child-generated noise and insanity?

Bandanas are also a necessity when tough love is called for. Sadly, in this day and age there is no other alternative for certain little varmints except to gag and hog-tie them. Some even require delivery to the sheriff.

DID YOU KNOW?

EARLY BANDANAS WERE OFTEN BLUE, BROWN, GRAY OR BLACK—NOT RED. THE FIRST RED DYES USED WERE UNEVEN AND FADED EASILY. EUROPEAN MANUFACTURERS DIDN'T GET RED DYES RIGHT UNTIL THE 1800s.

BANDANAS AND THE PAISLEY PATTERN BOTH HAVE ORIGINS IN INDIA. BOTH BECAME POPULAR IN ENGLAND DURING THE SAME TIME PERIOD. PAISLEY REMAINS A COMMON PATTERN FOR BANDANAS.

BANDANAS CAN BE USED TO MEASURE LENGTHS. EACH SIDE IS 22 INCHES. THE DIAGONAL IS 31 INCHES (ACTUALLY IT'S 31.112697 INCHES TO THE 6TH DECIMAL PLACE, BUT 31 INCHES IS CLOSE ENOUGH FOR GOVERNMENT WORK).

MORE COWBOYS THIS WAY ➡

D'YOU SAY YOU'RE LOOKING FOR MORE PERSONAL DANGER AND EXCITEMENT AS A COWBOY? ANOTHER LONG CATTLE DRIVE IS OUT. BARBED WIRE AND SOD-BUSTIN' HOMESTEADERS CLOSED DOWN THE OPEN RANGE LONG AGO. THE COWBOY PACKED HIS BANDANA AND LIT OFF TO THE RANCH.

ROUNDUP

I hear they're short of help over at the Double D Ranch. It's roundup time and they need every cowboy and his bandana. They want top hands, but you'll do.

Dan and Dawn run the Double D. Nowadays it ought to be the Quintuple D, what with D'Wayne, Denise and D'dog, but that would be too mean to those poor calves come branding time. Anyway, it's a good outfit with good grub. Dan is as fair a man as you'll work for. Not many were able to keep going after the winter of '86, but Dan did. He knows his business and expects you to know yours. Mamas' boys need not apply.

Are you sure you know what you're getting into? A cowboy's life is just as hard as it always was. The pay still stinks, but at least a bunkhouse beats the bare ground on a rainy night. You can't do this job without getting your bandana dirty. If you think you're man enough for the job, go see Dan first thing in the morning. You did say you can ride a horse and know how to handle a bandana, right?

BRANDING TIME

Your definition of first thing in the morning isn't the same as Dan's. By the time you get to the roundup center, the hands have all spread out. You see dust rising in every direction. The cattle are being flushed out of every thicket and gully. The clots of dust grow into clouds as the cattle merge into a milling herd and are nudged towards the center.

"Shoot," you think, "the roundup's over." Hold on. Plenty of work is left if you still want a job.

As soon as the herd is settled down, the hands move into action. There are some of the neighbor's cattle mixed in that have to be sorted out. The rest are tallied. Then it's time to start branding the calves.

Your job is to be a flanker. D'Wayne cuts a calf and its mother from the herd, maneuvers around the protective mama and ropes the calf. You want to make a good first impression. As D'Wayne tows the balking calf toward the branding fire, you run over. In a flash you grab the calf by the scruff of the neck with one hand and reach over its back to grab its flank. You rotate the calf back over your knees and flip it onto its side. Oh, oh, you forgot your lash. You improvise and whip out your bandana. You quickly tie the legs together and then throw your hands up. You did it so fast you might have been in the money at the rodeo.

Unfortunately this does not make any points with the branding crew. Those hind legs need to be stretched backwards so the branding iron will be pressed against taut skin. You've wasted time. Don't do it again or Woody may not be careful about who gets branded.

For now, Big and Little (who's bigger) will do the flanking. You do the earmarking and castrating while Woody does the branding. Take these—excuse the expression—sheep shears. Pinch the left ear together lengthwise and cut a swallow fork. Now pinch the right the same way but cut a spear point. When the ears heal, the calf will look like it's got an arrow through its head. This whole herd ought to be comedians.

Right now, the calf doesn't think things are funny. When he's let up, he shakes his head and sends blood everywhere. Your bandana mops the blood off your face and hands whenever you have a spare second. It's good you wore a red one today.

You prove yourself to be a good worker. What you did earlier is forgotten. Woody offers to let you do the branding. There's a big hole in your glove, so you wrap the end of the branding iron with your bandana.

Work is drawing to a close. The boys are roasting some snacks on the fire and offer you a couple to taste. They're hot, so plop them in your bandana. They taste pretty good. "What kind of oysters did you say these were?"

The boys think you did a good job. You don't want to know what the calves think. Dan offers you a job if you want to stay on until the fall roundup.

Now that you are a regular hand, your bandana will see plenty of action. Whether it's a fallen fence rail, a broken gate or an out-of-whack thingamabob on the whatchamacallit, your bandana can hold things together for the time being until it can be fixed right.

If you find some ripe berries up by the spring, bundle them home in your bandana. Ever since that problem you had with carrying those eggs in your hat, you've learned there's less risk carrying things in your bandana.

Your bandana will do some of its best work for you when it's pulled up over the nose to cover the unpleasant odors that come with the job. As a greenhorn, you may need to use it this way when you are mucking out the stable. Maybe after a while you won't notice the aroma. But there are some smells you'll never get used to. The stench of death, the gas from a bloated cow, and the bunkhouse air after Bart takes off his boots will always put the bandana over your nose.

As time goes on, you get to be pretty good at what you're doing. You begin to think you can handle any job that's thrown at you. In fact, you're getting a little too big for your britches. The Swayze brothers have just brought some mustangs down off the San Rafael Swell and Dan needs a bronco buster. Here's your chance to show your stuff. Why do all the hands bring their bandanas and a stretcher?

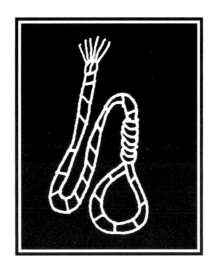

THE BANDANA AND THE BAD MAN

It's too bad you're laid up and couldn't come to town with us. Course, nobody expected you to get throw'd by A Few Minutes Past Lunch. I mean, she's not exactly Quarter Past Midnight. That hammerhead is one of the worst pieces of horseflesh the Swayze brothers ever brought to the ranch.

Anyway, me 'n' the boys went over to Kate's Kafe and we ran into the deputy who was in there on official duty. When he was through dunkin' his doughnut and flirtin' with Kate, the deputy had time on his hands, so he invited us back to the sheriff's office to see the sheriff's collection of criminal bandanas. What? No, the bandanas aren't criminals. Let's get something straight right off—bandanas don't do bad things; bad men do. The problem is that the bandana is just so darn useful. Just about every villain, thug and plug ugly has taken to the bandana just like flies to road kill. It seems every cowboy who's crossed over to the wrong side of the law took his bandana with him.

The sheriff has really put together one heck of a collection. He even has one of the first bandanas ever worn by a cowboy. Did you know the first cowboys were all bad guys? During the Revolutionary War, cowboys were not only rustlin' thieves, they were Tories. Worse yet, they were from New York. It don't seem right to think of thievin', traitor Yankees and cowboys at the same time, but it's true.

Folks still talk about the Yukon Jack gang that just 'bout ran things back in the '70s before law and order came to these parts. The sheriff's got a good number of their bandanas. The gang's mostly known for the bandana masks they wore while robbin' every stagecoach, bank and mail train that came by. Masked robbers are still around, 'cept now they hit armored cars instead of stagecoaches. Also, nowadays a lotta robbers use pantyhose instead of bandanas for masks. That sure helps the bandana's reputation, but it hasn't done much for the robber's image.

You can't believe all the bandanas we saw and all the crimes they were used in. Some murderers used bandanas as garottes. Burglers wrapped their hands with bandanas to break windows. There was even a bandana there that broke a window. How? It happened to tie a ransom note to a brick at the time.

Speaking of kidnappers, d'ya remember when that young widder got kidnapped? They have the bandana that blindfolded her and the ones that tied her hands and feet to the railroad tracks.

There's also a bandana blindfold some Polish, Danish, or some other Ish bank robber wore to try and rob a bank. Course he only used it once.

We also saw gags that had been used in all sorts of criminal activity, including marriage and child rearing.

The sheriff's even got a bandana that was 'bout to be used as a wick in a Molotov cocktail. A while back some crazy Russian rode into town—a gambler named Dusty Evsky or somethin' like that. Bill caught him hidin' an ace under his bandana durin' a poker game over at the saloon. The boys showed him the door but threw him out the window. That made the Evsky fella mighty sore. It's a good thing the boys saw him comin' back towards the saloon and stopped him before he could light that bomb.

This Evsky fella isn't the only one to ever hide somethin' in his bandana. All sorts of people who have more to hide than unsightly body parts or bad clothes have stowed small but valuable contraband in the folds of a bandana. Who's gonna check the bandana 'round yer neck for gold, jewels or whatever? No one'd think somethin'd be hidden in such an obvious place.

'Bout the saddest exhibit I saw was this bandana that some flimflam guy had used to impersonate a Boy Scout. How low can you go?

The sheriff even has a "how-to" exhibit to demonstrate how the bandana can be used all over a crime scene. A bandana can wipe off fingerprints or it can disguise a voice over the telephone.

The deputy says the sheriff plans to open a Museum of Bandana Crime some day that'll rival Scotland Yard's Black Museum. That'd sure put the town on the map. Course I don't know 'bout lettin' this stuff out to the public. It might give kids the wrong ideas. Come to think of it, I'm not sure I should've told you. From now on, you'd better keep your bandana where I can see it.

PICKUP TRUCK

Psst! Don't tell your horse, but the truth is you love your truck almost as much as Old Paint. And, if you value your life, don't tell your honey where she rates in this three-way contest.

Cowboy Cadillac, Utah Hardtop, whatever you call it—the pickup truck is a modern cowboy's necessity. A cowboy needs his bandana to keep his truck on the road.

Let's take a spin into town. Would you mind using your bandana to wipe the fog off the windows? Out here the radio reception's a little fuzzy, so there's a bandana on the antenna. When we go to the rodeo, we fly matching blue bandanas flag-like on the radio and CB antennas. Hopefully, some yahoo will think we are VIPs from the United Nations or something and let us park up close. If not, the bandanas still help us find our way back. A man can't get lost in the parking lot. It's not manly.

As we drive down Main Street, you can tell how each cowboy cares for his pickup by the way he uses his bandana. Since the first day he got his truck, old Carl has always had his bandana in hand to wipe every little smudge off the chrome.

But look at Vern's Ford. Talk about Fix Or Repair Daily! If he wipes anything with his bandana, it's just enough of a circle in the dirt to see out the windshield. The reason he probably doesn't use bandanas much for cleaning is that he's too busy using them elsewhere. See how he's duct taped that red bandana over his tail light? His right door is sprung and the inside handle is missing. A bandana, of course, pulls the door closed and then ties it shut. You know he'd probably tie his rear bumper on if he still had one. There are bandanas on his seat cover. His grandma might call

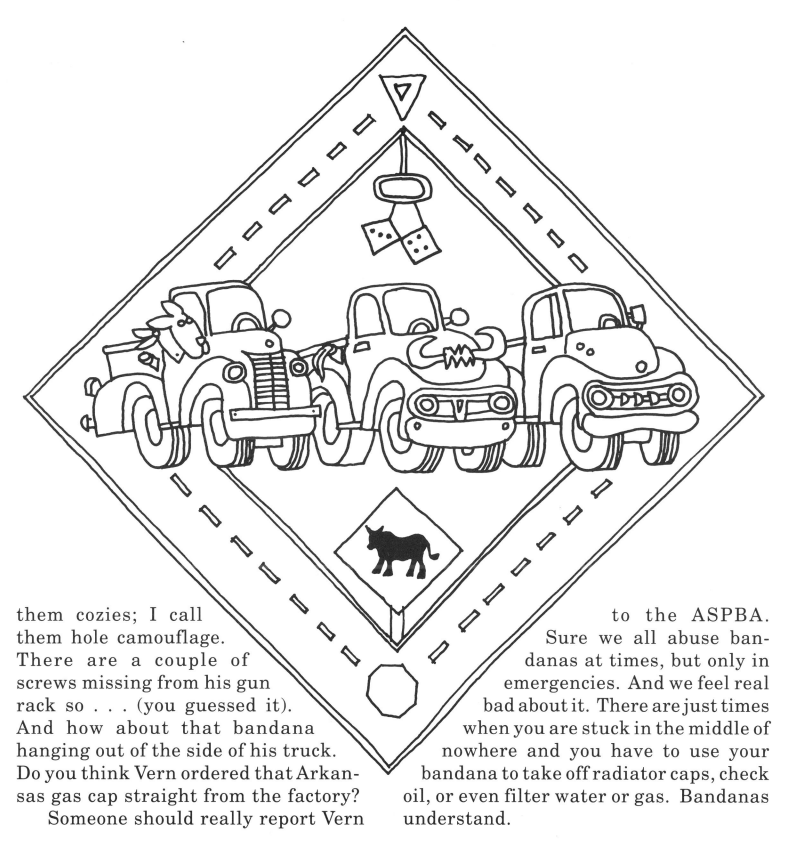

them cozies; I call them hole camouflage. There are a couple of screws missing from his gun rack so . . . (you guessed it). And how about that bandana hanging out of the side of his truck. Do you think Vern ordered that Arkansas gas cap straight from the factory?

Someone should really report Vern to the ASPBA.

Sure we all abuse bandanas at times, but only in emergencies. And we feel real bad about it. There are just times when you are stuck in the middle of nowhere and you have to use your bandana to take off radiator caps, check oil, or even filter water or gas. Bandanas understand.

GAMES FOR BORED COWBOYS

It's a slow day at the bunkhouse. Everybody's sick and tired of playing chess and checkers on Frank's checkerboard bandana. Frank just joined the Bandana-Game-of-the-Month Club. Next month he gets Candyland, every cowboy's favorite. So whaddya guys wanna do? How about some poker? Not with these cheaters.

Chet reminds us of the time the sheepherder came over. Chet took that sheepherder's bandana and knotted it around a wad of wool. Then he and Bart used their hats to bat it back and forth over the corral fence. Bad Mutton, they called it. No one wants to play.

The wind's picking up. Say, didn't Ben Franklin make a kite out of a bandana? Yeah, something like that, only his was silk. Our cotton bandanas are better for kite tails. Cal reminds us old Ben attracted lightning. That kind of nixes kite flying.

Seth is tossing his bandana up to watch it float down. We get to talking about how we used to make parachutes for toy soldiers. No one has any of those, but Cal has a pet mouse. Sure, the ASPCA wouldn't like it, but just tell the kids not to try it at home. If they can put a man on the moon, a few cowboys can soft-land a mouse. Now who's going to climb up on the roof?

Tom is twisting the radio dial. He finds a station, but it's playing something no cowboy should ever have to hear. Try as we might, no one can change the station. We are spellbound. An irresistible force begins to move unwilling lips—

"Bandana bandana bo andanna
banana panna fo fandanna
me my mo mandanna
ban—dan—na!"

The spell passes, but not the shame. No one speaks. There will be no more games. We resolve to read books.

THE MODERN BANDANA SPORTS WORLD

A Brit might say a bandana looks sporting. We never would.

Anyone who works up a sweat doing aerobics, lifting weights, running, bicycling, or playing racquetball, tennis, basketball, football, baseball, softball, rugby, soccer, volleyball, or any other sport or activity you can name wears a bandana. A bandana tells others, "I'm tough. I put out 100%." Chess players, dart throwers and their ilk may wear bandanas, but don't be fooled. They just wear them for effect. Scientists are still searching for the connection between bowling and bandanas.

A bicyclist who rides to work will use a bandana to tie a pant leg out of the way of the chain. Other bicyclists wrap bandanas on handlebars for comfort and color.

Paramilitary paintball soldiers are out of uniform without camo-bandana headwear.

A skier uses a bandana to protect the face from bitter cold. Bandanas tied to spare ski poles can be used as practice slalom gates.

Bandanas are just right for a game of frontier flag football in the park.

Bandanas were once a part of championship boxing. Before fancy custom shorts came into use, each boxer would tie a different-colored bandana around his waist so his fans in the cheap seats could identify him. Supporters could wave bandanas of the same color to cheer their man on.

And, of course, the bandana is instantly identified with the ultimate athlete—the rodeo cowboy.

BANDANA CHALLENGE #1

SAY THIS 101 TIMES:

BANANA BANDANA . . .

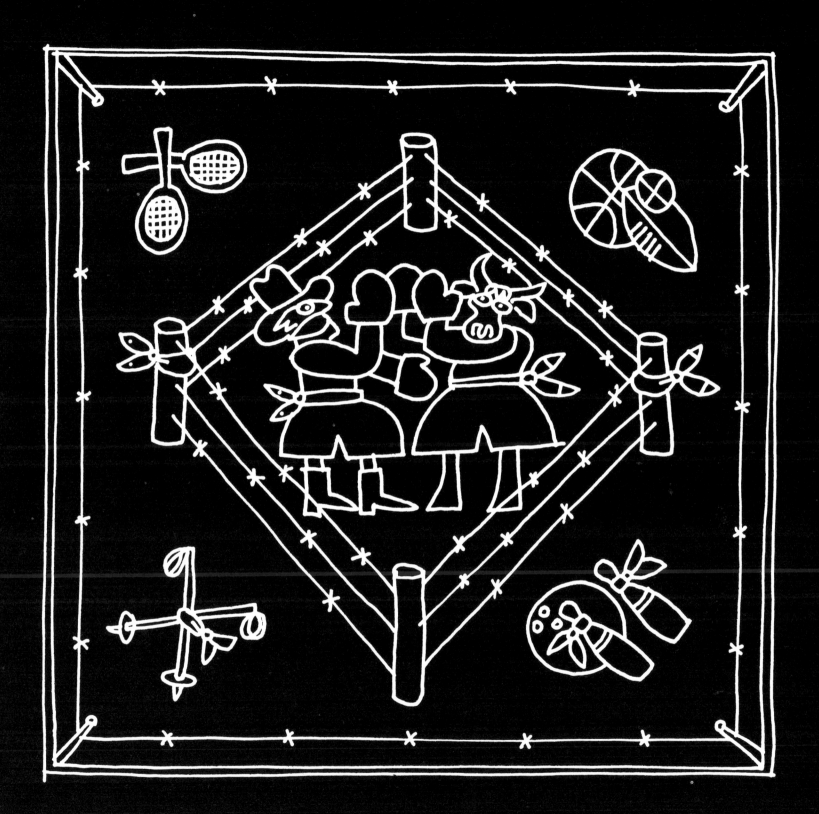

OTHER GAMES
For Very Drunk Cowboys

Nothing is more manly than bull fighting. Even in those silly tight, short britches, those toreadors are so macho. But they ain't got nothing on us. Rodeo clowns fight bulls with bandanas. So can we. There's a bull over there in the corral. Well, he's not a bull yet, but he still has all the plumbing to be one someday. Come on, either you fight him or Amos's pit bull. Here's a red bandana. You go first.

THE GAMES OF THE XXI BANDANIAD

Right now you could just kill your brother-in-law, Leonard. How did you let him sucker you into being in charge of the kids' games at the county fair? Sly Leonard had such a sob story. But now Barney has told you Leonard stuck you with the monsters so he wouldn't have to do it.

The little buckaroos all drift in. The rodeo will start in two hours, but what do you do until then? No one told you to bring any games, just to be in charge of them. You'd better think fast.

You notice the kids are dressed for the rodeo and each wears a bandana. Of course—the bandanas! If you start off by pairing them up and tying their left wrists together for Indian knife fighting, your problems will be cut in half. But then you realize that there is law and order in this town, if not justice, and you would never get away with it. Instead you settle for a three-legged race. They love it.

You follow up the race with some games. The little kids get in a circle while one child, bandana in hand, walks around saying, "I've gotta little doggie and he won't bite you. . . ." The bigger kids split into teams and play steal-the-flag and then grab-the-bacon.

While they're busy, you rummage around and find a leftover *piñata*, a rake handle, and some old political convention signs. First, the kids are blindfolded with their bandanas and they swat at the *piñata*. Meanwhile, you set up a Democrat donkey sign for the blindfolded buckaroos to pin a bandana tail on. The kids want to play the game with other signs. You guess it's fair to pin the nose on the G.O.P. elephant, but you have to draw the line. You tell Johnnie, "I know your dad said the governor is a jackass, but we aren't going to pin a tail on him."

You notice a friend over by the livestock pens. He agrees to bring a lamb, a calf, and a pig over to the show ring. You tie bandanas to their tails and offer the kids $5 for each bandana. Bedlam ensues. The parents had better not mind a little mud and manure on their darlings.

The time is almost up, but you need one more game. You find a sack of alfalfa pellets in a corner and make some bandana bean bags. You wish sly Leonard were around for the target. You remember the governor. It's a bit much to call him a jackass, but he sure is a big mouth. You cut the appropriate-sized oral opening on the gov's sign and the kids let fly.

The announcer says the rodeo is about to begin. The buckaroos run off to find whatever parents haven't hid themselves well enough. Now it's time for hide-and-seek with just you and sly Leonard.

THE MAGIC OF THE BANDANA

Are things slow at the saloon or church social? If a cowboy can't liven things up, nobody can.

Cowboys always brag about being magic in the saddle. Cowgirls practice bandana fashion magic. But not many know that a fair number of their brethren are skilled in bandana magic. A jackrabbit hops out of a full beaver ten-gallon hat just as easily as out of a silk top hat.

Would you like to join the Cowboy Magic Guild? First swear by your bandana you will never tell a soul what you are about to learn.

What's the secret? It's all fake!

Now you need a trick to get started fooling your friends and neighbors.

TRICK #1—BREAKING THE BANDANA RINGS

Before you are in front of your audience, lay your bandana flat and tie two opposite corners together with a square knot. Lay the knot in the middle of the bandana, and roll the bandana up to hide the knot. Put the bandana in your back pocket, but have one end sticking out.

Show time! Ask for someone's bandana. Tie two of its corners together with a square knot. Then pull the bandana from your back pocket, thread it through the circle formed by the stranger's bandana and tie a false knot in your bandana (see the bandana diagram to learn how to tie a false knot). Everyone will think you've tied another square knot.

Put the interlinked bandanas in your Stetson. Say some suitable cowboy mumbo jumbo. Reach back in the hat and pull out the stranger's bandana. Toss it to someone and have them check the knot.

Reach back in your hat, find the real knot, and lift the bandana out to show it is still knotted in a ring.

Golly!

AND OUR NEXT TRICK . . .

RAISING A BARN WITH A BANDANA

You've been promising your horses a new barn for years, and now it's time for you and your bandana to make good on that promise.

Before you start back to the ranch with the lumber, be sure your red bandana is tied on the longest piece. You may want to tie another bandana 'round your forehead, else you'll be mopping the honest sweat off'n your brow all day. If you make a double triangle fold and tie the open corners to your belt loops, your bandana will work as a nail apron.

Need a third hand to hold a stud while you nail it? Lash it. Ready to raise the walls? Its your job to pull on the rope, but you forgot your gloves. No problem. Wrap a bandana around each palm for a better grip and to avoid rope burn. Don't forget to hang a red bandana on every low beam.

Shoot, is it lunchtime already? Your buttercup brought a picnic lunch covered by a bandana to keep the flies off. She sits on one bandana and has another on her lap as a napkin and fly swatter. If you were a little smoother at the trough, you wouldn't need yours tied like a bib.

Time to get back to work. Damn! Why'd that hammer think a thumb looked like a nail? Wrap the thumb with your bandana and keep working. No time for feeling sorry 'bout yourself. Daylight's burning—and how! That water-soaked bandana sure feels good on the back of the neck.

With a little help from friends and neighbors, the barn is up. It's time to celebrate and have them over for a barn dance. Don't forget to wear your best bandana for a wild night of two-steppin' and square dancin'.

What's that, Mrs. O'Leary? The barn's on fire?! Quick, tie bandanas over the horses' eyes and get them out of there! Hold one over your mouth to help you breathe.

Now wipe the tears off your buttercup's cheeks and go to bed. There's a lot of work waiting tomorrow.

BANDANAS AND ROMANCE

There's a dance tonight at the T-Hat Ranch. You have never had butterflies like this before. Ever since Nellie dropped her bandana there in the feed store and you picked it up, you haven't thought of anything else. Until she did that, you were too shy or stupid to notice her. It's a good thing she knows how to send a message. Enjoy it. It'll probably be the last clear message she'll ever send.

You want to look your best. Your bandana does last-second boot-dusting and buckle-polishing duties. Do you think anyone will notice the red bandana on the right ankle and the blue one on the left? Well, you have to have a way to tell left from right. They stay.

Just before you leave, you pick her a pretty bouquet of flowers and tie it with a nice bandana.

It's time to call for Nellie. The pickup is as clean as it will ever be. You keep a bandana in your hand as you go up to her door. Wipe the nervous sweat off your hand before you shake hands with her father. Cover up that nervous cough and smile.

Nellie is wonderful. She breaks the ice by telling you her troubles getting ready. She ran out of tissues and had to blot her lipstick on her bandana. Luckily, the colors match perfectly.

A dance has never been so much fun. It ends way too soon, but not before you know you are head over heels in love with this girl.

On the way to her door, Nellie turns and plants a kiss on your cheek. Shy cowboy that you are, you blush and say good night.

As soon as you have driven out of earshot, you let out a rebel yell. Use your bandana to wipe off the lipstick before you get home. If anyone asks, you had a pretty good time, you guess.

DANCE

Cowboys and their bandanas have always loved to dance. When the West was too raw for sufficient female partners, cowboys figured out a way around that problem. They took turns tying a bandana on their arms to signify that they were suitable dance partners. Snicker all you want. Despite all the sick perversions neurotic Freudians may wish to insinuate here,

isn't it possible that these guys just wanted to have some clean fun? Remember, dancing was a major entertainment back then and played a different cultural role than it does today.

Bandanas are still dancing today at cowboy clubs and elsewhere. Who can forget that bandana dance bit in *Urban Cowboy*? City slickers slip on a bandana and are instantly ready to do-si-do at the square dance (or so they think). The bandana is also a great prop for doing the twist if you are in a '60s time warp.

Bandanas have been dragged by city kids to plenty of dances which would never have been approved by cowboys. Rock, funk, slam, rap, even—heavens no!—disco.

The bandana has also been appropriated by the illegitimate girlie shows. One report goes as follows:

'Twas once a cowgirl named Anna,
Did the dance of a single bandana.
The cowboys stampeded,
For the bandana she needed,
Was wider than all of Montana.

FROM A MODERN COWBOY'S DIARY

Dear Diary, as you know I am one lonesome cowpoke. I am so tired of the meat-market scene. There is no way I'll ever meet a nice girl by hanging around cattle auctions. The local watering holes attract flies, not real women.

This morning I read some advice Dear Gabby gave to some city guy who wasn't meeting girls either. She said to try looking in places other than bars. She suggested museums and such. Well it just so happened that the paper also had an article about a major exhibition of western art just down the road.

Now, I have to admit my tastes in art lean towards dogs playing poker or Elvis and the Duke together forever on black velvet, but I'm willing to try anything once.

I drove into the city and, boy, was I surprised when I got to the museum. A big crowd full of all types of people was there. "Uh, oh," I thought, "just what is western art?" Right away I knew these were paintings of cowboys because the guys wore bandanas. I had seen some of them before on calendars and such, but up close and personal they were something else.

I was standing in front of this Charles M. Russell painting, with my mouth open a little, when I got bumped. When I turned to see who bumped me, I saw the cutest little thing with a red bandana in her reddish-brownish hair staring at Charlie Russell's picture just like I was.

"Nice painting," I said.

"Beautiful," she replied. "It's one of my favorites by Russell. It speaks to me."

I started listening real hard, but no luck. "Well," I thought, "if you can't dazzle them with brilliance, baffle them with B.S." I answered, "It's almost screaming from where I stand. By the way, what's the name of this one?"

"*A Tight Dally and a Loose Latigo.*"

I was in luck, this was the one thing I knew.

"Did you know a dally is a half hitch a cowboy puts on his saddle horn after he ropes a steer, and a latigo is a strap that adjusts the saddle?"

"I kind of got the picture," she said. "Do you know what is the best part of the painting? It's Russell's use of that red bandana on the cowboy's neck. Bandanas are perfect for artists. They are a concentration of color that naturally draws the eye's attention. Do you see how Russell puts it at the apex of the triangle of action? From the bright bandana you follow the lariat leg of the triangle down to the ornery steers. The other leg of the triangle goes down to the nose of the cowboy's horse. Look at how the horse twists against the lariat's force on the slipping saddle. At this moment the cowboy and his bandana are still on top, still in control of the steer and the horse. But what will happen next? Can't you feel the dangerous excitement?"

"Huh?" I thought. "Exactly," I said.

"Let me show you another example of bandanas in art. Here, look at this. Remington's *A Dash for the Timber* uses bandanas for maximum effect. You can feel the wind pushing the bandanas. You see the speed. Look at the fluid motion of the whitish bandana into the blue dotted one, then the red one and finally the powder blue one. They all make a line which points back at the danger. The bandanas really add to my understanding of the desperation of these men."

I know it sounds crazy but she was starting to make sense. When I said, "I see," I was really beginning to.

Needless to say, we enjoyed the whole exhibition together. Of course, most all of the paintings had a bandana or two in them. When it was over I asked her out to dinner. She accepted. On our way she asked, "So, which was your favorite?"

"The one with the bandana," I replied.

BANDANA ART RULE #1
A BANDANA AROUND A HOWLING COYOTE'S NECK IS *NOT* SOUTHWESTERN ART.

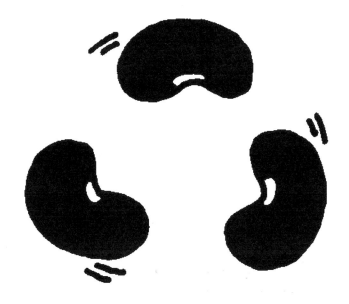

DINNER

The steak house we went to was nice and clean, the kind of place real people go to. It was perfect for continuing our conversation.

"I really love bandanas," she said.

"I hadn't noticed," I lied.

"I think the bandana can be used as a metaphor for what's good in Western civilization. Things like hard work, ingenuity and boldness come to mind. Have you ever taken the time to really look at bandanas? Their patterns and colors are always interesting. They aren't boring like life so often is. Bandanas not only do their jobs, they do them with style."

I was starting to feel something inside me and it wasn't heartburn. The jukebox was playing Merle Haggard's "Red Bandana." Just like Merle said, she had a red bandana around her *auburn* hair. That was a lot better than saying reddish-brownish. Thanks, Merle. And she really did look like she ought to be someone's wife somewhere. Hopefully here.

As dinner ended I said, "I'd like you to come see my bandana collection sometime."

Her eyes lit up. "How about now? Either your place or mine. I know a few tricks you might like, especially some with knots."

We couldn't leave fast enough.

THE DRIVE TO HER PLACE

It turned out she had a place in town, so we decided to go there. It's a good thing, too. My place was a mess. Besides, if this led to that, well, you know. Anyway, I've got all those pictures and stuff around that don't encourage things. First, there's the picture of Mom, and then there's the cross she brought back from her pilgrimage. Mary Anne and I haven't been an item for a long time, but I kept her picture. And I never feel like I measure up in these situations with the Duke looking at me. Shoot, by the time I'd had all of them covered up, there wouldn't have been any bandanas left for those tricks she promised.

Now, I'm not naive or anything, but I haven't exactly seen the whole world. I've heard the guys at the pool hall talk about this "tie me up, tie me down" stuff. Now really! To bed posts? Shower curtain rods? Railroad tracks? With bandanas?

There are just some things a bandana should not do, but it seems like it does them pretty well. This was getting too strange. "This isn't anything I'd do," I said to myself. Well . . .

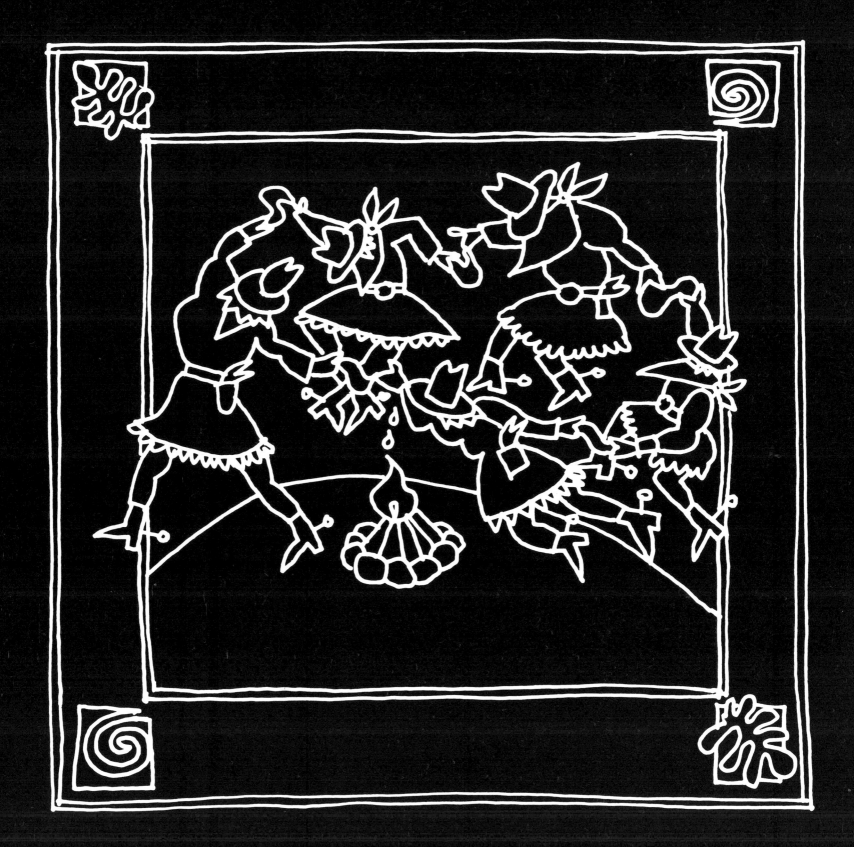

HER PLACE

She opened her door and we entered the Temple of the Bandana.

"I believe the bandana belongs in every part of our lives," she said.

I believed she believed it.

We talked for hours about darn near every subject in the world and how bandanas fit in the equation of most of them.

She continued my art education. "Bandanas have been in art since the 1700s. All sorts of common people are depicted wearing them. Let me show you a picture of the painting *Brook Watson & The Shark* by J. S. Copley. Most people look at the shark. I look at the bandanas on the sailors' necks."

She turned the pages of her art book. "Look at this self-portrait of Vincent van Gogh. For a guy who supposedly knew how to use bright colors, he missed the mark here by not wrapping his head with a bandana. Of course, he was crazy by the time he painted this one."

She pointed to a painting above her fireplace. "This is my most prized treasure. Few art historians will admit that Henri Matisse visited the American West when he was young and was heavily influenced by cowboy art. This painting is called *Dance of the Red Bandanas* and is from his lost American collection. When he returned to France he found that the critics only took paintings of nude women seriously, so he redid the work and renamed it *Dance*.

"I've heard rumors that Picasso had a bandana period. Although that has never been confirmed, I believe it. I mean, look at his daughter Paloma's scarf business. Where do you think she got the idea from?"

We took a break from the intellectual side of the bandana and used one to solve a scientific mystery of the ages—how to cut a Moon Pie exactly in half.

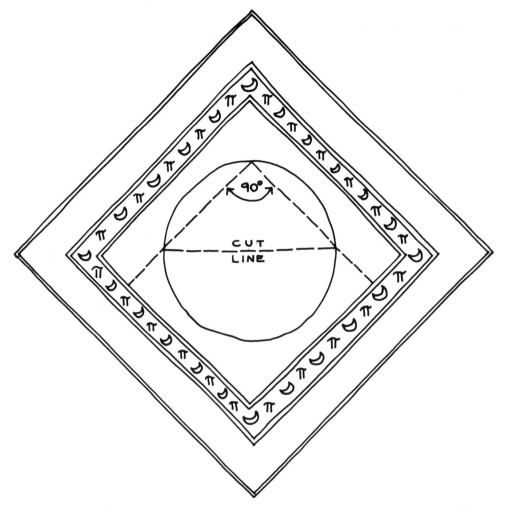

SOLVING THE MOON-PIE RIDDLE

Siblings everywhere have fought and died in the struggle to cut a Moon Pie exactly in half. Prescientific children had to use the "rule of pie"—one cuts and the other chooses first. This created rough but not exact parity.

Famed cowboy arithmetician Kay "Archimedes" Laursen came upon the solution one day in an advanced-geometry seminar. "Eureka!" he cried, but his was no gold strike. It was better.

A Moon Pie is a circle. Every corner of a bandana is a right angle (90°). Stretch part of the bandana over the moon pie with one corner of the bandana on the edge of the moon pie. You will see the bandana crosses the edge of the Moon Pie in two other places. Mark these two places and cut a straight line between the two for perfect halfsies. How does it work? You have made a right triangle. The 90° angle of a right triangle subtends an arc of 180°, which is exactly half of a circle.

Today's cowboys don't major in range science for nothing.

THE PHILOSOPHICAL BANDANA

STUMP YOUR FELLOW MENSANS WITH THESE, PARTNER.

1) A) IF A BANDANA FALLS ON THE OPEN RANGE AND NO ONE IS THERE, DOES IT MAKE A SOUND?

   B) IF A BANDANA FALLS ON THE OPEN RANGE AND SOMEONE IS THERE, DOES IT MAKE A SOUND?

2) WHAT IS THE SOUND OF ONE BANDANA CLAPPING?

IF YOU FIND THESE INTRIGUING, WATCH FOR THE NEW BOOK *BEING AND BANDANANESS.*

BACK AT HER PLACE

After we finished our Moon Pie snack, she said, "Oh, there are a couple of other things about art that I wanted to show you.

"I love art, but there are so many works that would be so much better if they had a bandana or two in them." She reached for another book.

"Here's *The Birth of Venus* by Botticelli. He uses her hair to cover her up a bit, but she should be holding a bandana to shield her other parts. Botticelli could never paint feet. Those things really need to be covered up with something."

"There are a lot of preachers who'd be happy to plaster bandanas all over these nudies," I said as I flipped through her book. "Wow, look at this statue of David!"

"Now that you bring up religion," she replied, "I believe Adam and Eve first wore bandanas. Fig leaves just aren't believable."

"Religion, censorship and bandanas go back a long way," I guessed.

IS IT TRUE?

ELVIS HAD A BANDANA CAPE?

PHARAOH WORE THE FIRST BANDANA?

THE GRAND FINALE

It was getting late. We had passed through nearly every topic known to man and bandana—history, philosophy, music, films, television and a few others—whizzed over my head.

"Oh, I almost forgot why you came up here," she said. "Do you still have time?"

"I'll make time."

She led me to another room. It was dark.

"Just a minute while I change. Okay, are you ready?"

Boy, was I.

A light went on—actually it was a spotlight fixed on her. She held a bandana over her head like a bonnet.

"I can't pay the rent!" she said in a high voice. Then she rotated 180°. She lowered the bandana to her upper lip to fashion a sinister moustache and dropped her voice to a low sneer.

"You must pay the rent!"

Back to the first pose. "I can't pay the rent!"

Then back and forth she went until not another drop of dramatic tension could be squeezed out of the scene. Finally, she held the bandana to her neck, hero style, and faced front stage.

"I'll pay the rent!"

"My hero!"

So this is what she had in mind. The night had certainly been a slice, but now it was time to cut out.

"Gee, I've got to go," I mumbled.

"Wait, there's more," she called after me.

As I was closing the door, I heard her calling, "Didn't you want to see my knots? Here's a bowline, a sheep shank and a clover hitch.

WILL YOU CALL ME?"

THE BANDANA IN HOLLYWOOD

Don't call movies "movies." They are "films" or "motion pictures." Western films are more properly called "oaters" or "horse operas."

There were too many cowboy bandanas used in oaters to address them all here. But here are a few observations.

Hollywood has shown us that a cowboy would be naked without his bandana. How many scenes showed a cowboy still wearing his bandana while he bathed in a lake or a tin tub? The red union suit was optional.

The theory of bandana relativity states that the bigger the hero, the bigger the bandana. Prime examples are the Duke and Marshall Dillon.

Nobody ever wore a bandana better than the Duke. How did he manage to tie it on the side and still get the full triangle spilling color down the front of his shirt? Did this bandana style come in handy after a hard day of triumphing over evil when the school marm invited him over for spaghetti?

Back in the good ol' days (you know, when you could take your mom to the movies without blushing and covering her eyes), before Sam Peckinpah brought us *The Wild Bunch,* our heroes were only winged during gunfights. The bad guys were such lousy shots they should have known they didn't stand a chance. But the idiots never gave up peaceful-like. Instead of laying down their shootin' irons like they were told, they always forced Roy, Tom or Rex to shoot the desperadoes' guns clean out of their hands. This type of action held down the blood and gore. It also held up the demand for bandana slings.

One final thought for cowboys who dream of heading down the trail to stardom. Keep a bandana tied as a spare handle on your broken suitcase before you get to the bus stop. That may keep you from dumping your underwear out when you put your suitcase in the overhead rack of the Greyhound to Phoenix. It wouldn't make a good impression on that gorgeous blonde. What's her name?

THE BANDANA AND FOREIGN RELATIONS

THE JAPANESE LOVE THE AMERICAN COWBOY. THE TRADE DEFICIT WOULD BE EVEN HIGHER IF JAPANESE TOURISTS DIDN'T WANT TO COME TO THIS COUNTRY TO RIDE A HORSE AND BUY COWBOY CLOTHES AND BANDANAS.

NOT EVERYONE KNOWS THAT THE JAPANESE HAVE MADE A MAJOR CONTRIBUTION TO THE CULTURE OF THE AMERICAN WEST. THE CLASSIC FILM *THE MAGNIFICENT SEVEN* WAS BASED ON *THE SEVEN SAMURAI*. COME TO THINK OF IT, THE JAPANESE HAVE BEEN WEARING BANDANA-STYLE HEADWEAR FOR CENTURIES. DO WE HAVE MORE IN COMMON THAN WE THINK? AH SO!

THE JAPANESE ARE ALSO BUYING UP RANCHES. RANCH HANDS WOULD BE SMART TO PICK UP A LITTLE CONVERSATIONAL JAPANESE, AND MAYBE SOME JAPANESE HANDICRAFT SKILLS WOULD HELP WHEN THE NEW BOSS-SAN COMES AROUND.

BANDANA ORIGAMI

ANIMAL BANDANA TIPS

IF USED PROPERLY, A PET IS AN APPROPRIATE ACCESSORY TO A BANDANA.

A DOG MAY WEAR A BANDANA FOR A COLLAR. A POTBELLIED PIG MAY NOT.

A CAT MAY CHASE, BUT NEVER CATCH, A DANGLED BANDANA.

A BANDANA MAY BE THREADED THROUGH THE GILLS OF ALL THE TROUT YOU CATCH. DO NOT TRY THIS WITH A SHARK.

DO NOT ATTEMPT TO USE A RED BANDANA FOR SPANISH-STYLE BULLFIGHTING WITH A PIT BULL NAMED "KILLER."

BANDANAS WITH THE SMILEY FACE PATTERN MAY BE KNOTTED INTO PET TOYS OR USED TO COVER OR LINE BIRD CAGES.

BANDANA CLUB MEMBERSHIP QUESTIONNAIRE

1) IS THERE SOMETHING ABOUT A BANDANA THAT IS FRIENDLY OR FAMILIAR TO YOU?

2) DO YOU TALK TO YOUR BANDANA?

3) DOES YOUR BANDANA TALK TO YOU?

4) DID YOU GROW UP WATCHING YOUR HEROES WEAR BANDANAS IN WESTERNS?

5) AS A CHILD, DID YOU WEAR A BANDANA WITH YOUR COWBOY HAT AND CAP GUN SIX-SHOOTERS?

6) DID YOUR GRANDFATHER CARRY A BANDANA IN HIS POCKET?

7) DID YOUR MOTHER WEAR A BANDANA:

A) TO CLEAN THE HOUSE?

B) WHILE CRUISING DOWN THE ROAD WITH THE 4/60 AIR CONDITIONING (4 OPEN WINDOWS, 60 MPH) CRANKED UP?

8) AS A CHILD, DID YOU EVER PACK A BANDANA, PUT IT ON A STICK AND RUN AWAY FROM HOME (AT LEAST UNTIL IT GOT DARK)?

9) DURING THE 1960s THE BANDANA WAS USED AS AN ARTICLE OF CLOTHING ALL OVER THE BODY BY THE FLOWER CHILDREN. WAS THIS A LEGITIMATE EXPANSION OF BANDANA USE?

10) Do you consider a bandana to be:

    A) a practical item?

    B) a fashion piece?

    C) a social statement?

    D) all of the above?

    E) none of the above?

11) How many times a week do you wear or use a bandana?

    A) How many ways?

12) Does the bandana come and go with popular fads, or is it a permanent part of the American style?

13) Do you sweat, sneeze or slobber?

14) When you wear a bandana, do you:

    A) feel the spirit of the American cowboy in you?

    B) find it easier to attract members of the opposite sex?

    C) think more clearly?

    D) act more decisively?

    E) leap tall buildings in a single bound?

    F) know how to bring about world peace?

15) Can you score 100% on the following quiz?

BANDANA QUIZ

1. **THE BANDANA:**

   A. WAS ONCE A KEY PART OF INTERNATIONAL TRADE WITH INDIA;

   B. CAUSED BRITISH IMPERIALIST EXPANSION INTO INDIA;

   C. STARTED THE INDUSTRIAL REVOLUTION IN BRITISH PRINTED TEXTILES;

   D. MADE COTTON KING;

   E. ALL OF THE ABOVE.

2. **WHAT BECAME PROFITABLE CONTRABAND FOR SMUGGLERS IN ENGLAND AFTER THE CALICO ACTS OF 1701 AND 1702?**

3. **WHAT DID COLONIAL MILITIAMEN WEAR INTO BATTLE DURING THE REVOLUTIONARY WAR?**

4. **WHAT DID DANIEL BOONE AND OTHER TRAILBLAZERS TAKE EVER WESTWARD TOWARD ITS MANIFEST DESTINY?**

5. **WHAT EVENT WOULD YOU LEAST LIKE TO SEE AND/OR HEAR?**

   A. BANDANAS ACROSS AMERICA.

   B. A BANDANA-CLAD FAT LADY END AN OPERA.

   C. ALL OF THE ABOVE.

6. **W**HAT WOULD YOU TIE TOGETHER INTO A ROPE IN ORDER TO ESCAPE OUT OF A HIGH WINDOW IN THE EVENT OF FIRE IN A BANDANA FACTORY?

7. **W**HAT SYMBOL OF THE **A**MERICAN **W**EST HAS ITS ORIGINS IN THE **F**AR **E**AST?

8. **W**HAT **E**NGLISH WORD IS CLOSELY RELATED TO THE **H**INDI WORDS *BANDHNU* AND *BANDHANI*?

9. **I**F YOU SEE A POLITICIAN WEARING A BANDANA AT A BARBECUE, SHOULD YOU:

   A) SHAKE HIS/HER HAND?

   B) VOTE FOR HIM/HER?

   C) REPORT BANDANA ABUSE TO THE PROPER AUTHORITIES?

10. **M**ATCH WHEN THE FOLLOWING NECKPIECES WERE FIRST WORN BY **A**MERICANS.

BANDANA	1940S
FOUR-IN-HAND TIE	1740S
BOLO TIE	1880S

THE BANDANA QUEST

It's just about time to go our separate ways. It's been a pleasure to have you along for the ride. Now, don't get all teary-eyed. Think of this as the beginning, not the end. Now that you're a member of the Cowboy Bandana Club, it's your turn to carry the torch. See what your bandana can do for you and what you can do for your bandana. Be sure to take pictures of what you do and send them to me.

For starters, see how many things you can give a western flair to by simply adding a bandana. How about your neighbor's lawn flamingos? That statue in the city park could use a little color besides pigeon white. The guy sleeping on that bench will appreciate the gift.

Once you have mastered stationary objects you might want to try to put a bandana on something that moves. If you are still in the park with the statue, you could try the pigeons and squirrels. Too fast, eh? Maybe you'd better try domesticated animals. A mutt always looks good in a bandanna, but that's too easy. Challenge yourself. No one has ever been able to make anything worthwhile out of a poodle, but you and your bandana can sure try. Another challenge will be to keep a bandana on a snake.

Humans are fair game. Be sure to obtain Mama's permission before you make a junior ranger out of her "little precious." Otherwise you may be doing something you won't want to do with a bandana—eating it.

It is your special duty to spread the cowboy bandana faith among the young. We've got to help these kids grow up with the right values like courage, honesty, loyalty, independence and resourcefulness. Look at what a bandana did for Teddy Roosevelt. As a child, T. R. was a pampered weakling who dressed like a girl. But once he put on a bandana, he was off to the Badlands to become a real cowboy. The next thing you know, T. R. and his bandana were charging up San Juan Hill. Bully!

It would be fun to take the cowboy bandana cross-country on a road trip. You'll have plenty of opportunities in every town. All those silly statutes and signs in front of roadside eateries and tourist traps alone should keep you busy. Don't forget to spread the cowboy bandana among the people you meet. The more stuffed the shirt, the greater the need for the cowboy bandana. Bonus points will be awarded for every bandana you can tie on a Boston Brahmin or Philadelphia lawyer. The entire city of New York could use a healthy dose of the cowboy bandana and what it stands for. If that place would clean up and calm down, cowboys would stop calling it the Big Road Apple.

There's no reason to stop at the Atlantic Ocean. The cowboy bandana is needed overseas. Imagine a large bandana on the Eiffel Tower. While in Paris do something about those stupid women's fashions. Hang bandanas on the mannequins in a snooty boutique. If you mistake the manager for a mannequin, just say, *"Pardon, Madame."* Sometimes it's so hard to tell the difference. Well, she could use one, too.

Keep moving eastward. How about a bandana on the Sphinx? He needs something to smile about.

Finally, return to the land of the bandana's birth, India. Maybe East can finally meet West through the bandana. Hindus may not like what we do to cows, but they'll love what we've done to bandanas.

The next guru who comes to America would win more cowboy converts if he wore a bandana turban.

Don't just cross the country, cross the cultural arts. Ballet has already tippeetoed into the bandana world with *Rodeo* and *Billy the Kid,* but wouldn't *Swan Lake* get a better reception in Abilene if the dancers wore bandana tutus? Classical music might seem a little less stuffy if the concertmaster used a bandana chin pad for his fiddle and the conductor wore a bandana instead of a white tie.

Cowboys and their bandanas have made their mark in nearly every movie genre except monster movies. Maybe Frankenstein's monster acted like he did because he was sensitive about those electrodes on his neck. Just think how the villagers would be amazed by the cowboy who singlehandedly tames the monster by giving him a bandana or two or 300 to hide his slight imperfections. Cowboy-horror flicks may cause the rebirth of "B" movies.

Few will ever be a cowboy. None will ever be what a cowboy has come to symbolize. But all can use the cowboy's bandana and be better for it. The spirit of the cowboy is in us all. It's your job to bring it out. Go forth, be fruitful and multiply the bandana's uses.

90

FAMOUS BANDANA SAYINGS

(OR THEY SOON WILL BE)

A BANDANA A DAY KEEPS THE DOCTOR AWAY.

GIVE ME BANDANAS OR GIVE ME DEATH.

I REGRET THAT I HAVE BUT ONE BANDANA TO
GIVE FOR MY COUNTRY.

FOUR SCORE AND TWENTY BANDANAS AGO . . .

DAMN THE TORPEDOES, FULL BANDANA AHEAD.

WHAT'S GOOD FOR **GENERAL BANDANAS** IS GOOD FOR **AMERICA**.

THE ONLY GOOD BANDANA IS A RED BANDANA.

PRAISE THE LORD AND PASS THE BANDANAS.

ON A BANDANA AND A PRAYER.

A FRIEND IN NEED NEEDS A BANDANA INDEED.

H.R.H. ELIZABETH II ALWAYS WEARS A FRUMPY SCARF OVER HER HAIR. SHOULD WE SEND HER A BANDANA AND LET HER JOIN THE CLUB?

 A) YES.

 B) NO.

☐ C) MAYBE.

Other western books from Gibbs Smith, Publisher:

Calamity and Belle: A Cowgirls' Correspondence
Belle Bendall and Calamity Wronsky, illustrations by Bill Schenck

The Insider's Country Music Handbook
Country Joe Flint and Judy Nelson

The Cowboy Boot Book
Tyler Beard, photos by Jim Arndt

Cowboy Boot Calendar 1994
photos by Jim Arndt

Cowboy Curmudgeon and Other Poems
Wallace McRae, illustrations by Clint McRae

Cowboy Engagement Calendar 1994
photos by Jim Arndt

Cowboy High Style: Thomas Molesworth to the New West
Elizabeth Clair Flood

Cowboy Poetry Cookbook
Cyd McMullen and Ann McMullen

Cowboy Poetry: A Gathering
edited by Hal Cannon

Don't Squat With Yer Spurs On!: A Cowboy's Guide to Life
Texas Bix Bender

Never Ask a Man the Size of His Spread: A Cowgirl's Guide to Life
Gladiola Montana

New Cowboy Poetry: A Contemporary Gathering
edited by Hal Cannon

Old-Time Cowboy Songs
book edited by Hal Cannon and cassette tape by the Bunkhouse Orchestra

Riders in the Sky
Ranger Doug, Too Slim and Woody Paul, with Texas Bix Bender